Beneath the Naked Sun

POETRY BY

Connie Fife

Sister Vision
Black Women and Women of Colour Press

ISBN 0-920813-59-3

Canadian Cataloguing in Publication Data
Fife, Connie, 1961-
Beneath the Naked Sun

Poems
ISBN 0-920813-59-3

I. Title

PS8561.I42B45 1992 C811'.54 C93-093074-6
PR9199.3.F43B45 1992

Cover photograph of a Kootenai Indian woman living near Windermere, British Columbia: Bettie Zinkan (Sidney, British Columbia)
Book design and production: Stephanie Martin
Proofreading: Jane Greer
Printed and bound in Canada by Union Labour

Published with the assistance of the Canada Council and the Ontario Arts Council.

Published by
Sister Vision
Black Women and Women of Colour Press
P.O. Box 217
Station E
Toronto, Ontario
Canada M6H 4E2

In honour of
my grandmothers
who have moved on
yet who always stay close.

To my son, Russell. This is for your gifts of constant inspiration, laughter and patience.

To all Native lesbians who struggle daily and whose visions give me strength.

To each Native writer who has blazed the trail before me. Your words are responsible for breaking the silence and ensuring that truth be written.

A special thanks to Stephanie Martin and Makeda Silvera whose encouragement and unending work at Sister Vision brought this collection into print.

Thank you.

Contents

These are the spirits

there are spirits flowing through my veins / some are old / others are young / there are women in my blood who scream loudly with contorted mouths / and men who drown in alcohol then beat those screaming / either way they live inside me and with determination have survived the howling / lived to tell of the blood-letting / those in my veins laugh when others might cry / uttering damn what a bad joke this has all become / it is those whose tears make up the dew that arrives with a new sunrise / there are men inside of me who are beaten by reality every day / and they love their women and weep at what they themselves have become / then there is my young trickster who can become a tree / or the young man who watches as i drive into the night / his hair is made of wind and swirls into the sky / there are young women living inside my chest and i ache with their pain on some days / sometimes they play / my hands touch the stars when they take flight / these same young women speak up in assemblies / they seep through my fingertips when i look back into my childhood / it is their arms that wrap themselves around my body when i cannot / old women house themselves in my caves / crawling out when i'm on my knees creating a river leading to their ocean / it is their hands which caress me when i find no warmth in my own / they give over to me their pasts in order to make a clearing in this jungle of asphalt / there are old women in my veins who surface only in the safety of my sleep / they pass on to me their visions at moments when i have none of my own/ these same women push me past survival and into resistance / there are spirits flowing through my veins / i know this because i am them / and when i am not i am becoming / these spirits are young and old / or neither / i know this because i interrupted them in the morning / then spent the day with them walking through my corridors/

DEAR WEBSTER

savage *(sav'ij) adj. without civilization; primitive; barbarous (a savage tribe) n. a member of a preliterate society having a primitive way of life; a fierce, brutal person.*

i am the one who talks with the mountains
when i am not sliding down the stream of its face /
i am the one who walks the streets late at
night despite the danger
believing that this land is mine to roam freely /
i am the one who carved a mask from a thick tree
then wore it /
i am the one who raises her arms to the sun
then takes flight on winds from the east /
i am the one who says "no more"
then leaves the man whose fists have reconstructed
my bones /
i am the one who defies the narrow definition of love
and loves another woman
and heals a nation in doing so /
i am the one who meeting after meeting turns
away when men misconstrue my words
and goes on /
i am the one whose stories take our collective
pasts into the future
and guarantees that not one day is left behind /
i am the one sleeping on sidewalks
who speaks to all my relations as the masses
hear only their own silence /
i am the one who cradles close to her breasts
small children
and women who were old before they were young /

I am the one who shoots fire into the veins of those
who cannot re-ignite their own sparks
then gives them the responsibility of stocking
the wood /
i am the one who talks to herself and hears
others answer
then writes it down so that the words remain in
my throat /
i am the one who demonstrates against forced
relocation
and uses a shotgun to carry the message clean home /
i am the one who watched as my children's hair
was cut
and cried and wept then screamed "return them" /
i am the one struggling to find her way back
i am the one who uses brushes to paint my resistance
on a canvas
then hangs my tapestry across the horizon /
i am the one whose son died of a.i.d.s. while a piece
of myself died each day and couldn't halt either
then buried my child /
i am the one who was raped by my father then
my uncle
and spent years hiding then decided to change it all
and used all my rage to castrate my memory of them
and healed myself with love /
i am the one who late at night screams and howls
and hears voices answer /
i am the one whose death was intended
and didn't die

dedicated to Beth Brant

Brick by brick

i have tried living your way,
approaching life from your
narrow perspective, using your
concepts of development for
my homeland, your notions
of how to make change...
these words you have given me
have assisted my gathering
of weapons with which to
fight back with...
daily bodily contact with
you has left abrasions
on my soul and the stench
of infected sores can be
smelt in your classrooms
while trying it your way
i in turn festered the puss
already running down my heart
while my thoughts came
to a full boil and recovery
became essential to my flight.
so unlike a doctor waiting in
the emergency ward at a hospital
i will not bandage my wounds nor
will i pop a new wonder drug.
instead i will take down your
institutional walls brick by brick,
planting in its place
a forest of knowledge and
an ocean of healing.

Oka on my mind

steel teeth scrape her scalp
while in their tracks
bleeding flesh separates from bone
overhead the blades whirl and
their sound inside creates a dust
storm of thought wound in a wind of fury
below the earth turns over and on a
hurricane of rage she travels to her
place of remembering only to be
greeted by the barrel of a gun
hard and black the cylinder finds
a place to rest against her forehead
while the roots of white peace
congeal in a pool at her feet
each word spoken becomes only another
puddle of blood in which to drown
the rebel sitting in her centre
finds no refuge from the burning eyes
so determined to witness a death
escape stands alone on a crumbling
mountain of boiling lava far
off in the distance of every yesterday
waiting for a tomorrow
absent of all weaponry

Muriel

I wanted to cradle your arm which shook
violently from drugs prescribed by whitemen
in long flowing white cloaks who deceived
the world into believing they knew best.
I wanted to give you back your memories
taken from you through years of shock treatment
that must have propelled your body into retreat.
I wanted to call you back into the sunlight
to take away the mist covering your eyes
stopping you from seeing your own beauty.
I wanted to scream into the sky for the abuse to
end in your lifetime so you could look
forward to your tomorrows without fear.
I wanted to be able to find the right words
so that your story would be told full of
the truth of who you are and where you are from.
I wanted to brush away the sadness that clouds
your view of the world then be able to change
the lies and distortion that line the universe.
I wanted to be able to say to you that I see
shimmering light despite all attempts
at blocking it out
I tried but there were not enough words.

Twisted tongues

this familiar language of yours
rings harshly against the silence of
this place changed now by your presence
and the words you have brought through
using an outsider's tongue

i have often wondered what it is
to be told to no longer speak
in the language of my origin was
not allowed to touch on the syllables
of my grandmothers   i know only of
the meaning of loss and what it is
to crave for that which you never had

i twinge not out of being inadequate at
the english spouting from your lips
could match you word for word
i react out of not being able to
speak with those women who sat
with me in the sweat lodge on the
eve of my first return home
here i was surrounded by their
prayers for the healing of my wounds
the mending of my heart   torn by
years of absence and forced assimilation

this class of yours bores me for i
do not desire to speak with the same
lack of meaning found in your words
i will sit patiently until the breeze

caused by your lecture has subsided and
the smell of your acidic breath leaves this room
i cannot respectfully
apologize for this desire in my
body to spit your words back where
they belong   instead my silence and
lack of attention is all i am left with
following years of living on the
borders of your world

dedicated to Ruth Ogalvie

Ronnie, because they never told you why

twenty eight years old
at an age where
to be told
is to understand
yet on this dark
night you are
locked in a
vice grip of racism
condemned by a court
system that leaves
rooms taking its
small barred cells
to the streets where
white men prowl
like starving dogs

not finding a guilty party
they settle
for the innocent
stopped
you question
their investigation
and
receive only their
special looks saved
for indians who believe
we never lost
the war of the west that
they are sure they
are still fighting

until our total annihilation
not one of us
is above suspicion

this time it is you
who is taken to
their station and
enclosed behind steel
obstructions released
early the following day
you are finally entitled
to knowledge of your crime
you are guilty of being
brown indian lesbian woman
you are criminal in
your nature because
you do not
believe in your guilt
like they do
will sign no confession
instead swearing to fight
back against a system
that wishes for your silence
and eventual death
though as long as you
do die they will
allow you to scream

you dare to walk down
sidewalks of cold concrete
alone deep into the night
in the belief that you

are entitled to be
anywhere on this continent
left to you by your
grandmothers and grandfathers
worse than this attitude
you travel where and
when you want

your skin is not white
and you say you are
proud to be
indian
prouder still of your
love for women
so you carry your head
raised always to the sun
back straight
you break all laws
by not lowering your
eyes to the stares of
white people
by not cowering in dark corners
meant for rats and alcoholics
safe in their drunken stupors

you are charged with
two counts of assault
and one of robbery
but not until you
have been hurled
against the police car
handcuffed

while they try to
steel your dignity
still you say you
will
fight back

how to be caged & never know it

get comfortable with the chains
cease to notice their chilling clutch

put up bars around your home
begin to feel safe within the metal

install an alarm system in your mind
so you can recognize beauty & destroy it

phone the police when your words are ineffective
encourage their billy clubs to bring your point home

turn off the television when humanity's face gets air time
that way you don't have meet their dark eyes

raise your voice when the conflict is in the same room
drain over drain out verbally suck in more air than you need

phone social services when their children confront injustice
so that the throne stays shiny and the children locked up

institutionalize the women the old the young the unborn
that way lineage doesn't have a hope & cannot occur

rape the women   make them ugly and grotesque
that way their children can be pushed aside without remorse

instill hate in all copper black bronze men
they can take your place you can watch the football game
on Sunday [after you've fucked the priest]

attack the earth with great urgency
being is empty without her/his mother's nurturance

kill every living animal not already extinct
the earth will have no reason to struggle

turn friendly plants into enemies give truth seekers alcohol
that way nothing is sacred including self

introduce subliminal thoughts of American pie
so that it looks more delicious than the sun
that way the heat can go out and no-one will care

dance on the graveyards of everyone's dead except your own
that way the neighbours have a pastime to look forward to
indulging themselves in

have a feast invite all your saints every last one
that way not one will be hungry or malnutritioned
crunch down on flesh barrel down on spirit
drain away drain away drain away
replace with man-made watering holes man-made
watering holes
drain away drain away drain away
don't stop don't stop
never meet inside yourself
never look in a mirror
never look in the water
never ponder stones story
never look to the clouds
never never love
never never acknowledge passion

never never feed truth
never never remember
never never recall
never never reclaim
never return to earth's centre
never taste your own blood
never taste your mothers
never stop
never falter
never quiver
never doubt

that way you can stay caged and
never
know it

a note concerning school
may 31 in the lord's year 1989

i am tired of a system
that guarantees full integration
without the accompaniment of
any form of freedom or the
allowance of the shape of dignity.
then again, i am exhausted at
having to repeat myself in
the first place...

you have locked in your
mind's eye a picture of me
and of how, precisely, i can
fit into your society.
your vision for me has existed
on this continent since 1492 and
since its birth i have told you
countless times, while under
various circumstances, that
i do not desire to become like you.
to do so would mean carrying your
burden of shame for the
trail of tears left in your tracks.

there. i did it again and
i am exasperated by my having
repeated myself one more time and
in return having to look at
your bloody hands...
you can plead with me to

wash them clean and to pick
away the still moist flesh
caked under your fingernails,
but do not be surprised
when i decline.

Communications class

if i drop out of your educational system
do not fool yourself that i have fallen
off the face of the earth and
am just another statistical write-off.
this act will cause you embarrassment and
i am familiar with the feeling of
being caught turning red in the face.
tomorrow if you do not find me, again,
dozing during another one of your lectures
do not think firstly that i have disappeared
amongst sheets of paper shelved in
a reference library....
instead picture me wide awake at 3:00 a.m.
throwing ink upon blank white squares
creating with your own language
a universal formula for change.

Untitled

an endless stream of unseen words,
cluttered within the cold
cement confines of walls.
story pulled from memory,
gathered into a moment of urgency,
to be spoken, to be moved towards
a new beginning in its retelling.
a metaphor thrown skyward,
determined to live,
examining the world through different eyes.
a poem born by its own desire to be heard,
longing to fill rooms with its warmth.
constant words birthing words,
creating from distorted language
clarity originating from that
most secret place where what is
spoken will leave behind
a trail of lightning

dedicated to Muriel Miguel

Stains

I

stained ochre earth mourned her past
    remembered woman's footsteps across
forest floor   down hillsides into eye
of opening where women gathered
in sanctuary   before the bloodlet
there was song   before the slaughter
the laughter of children rested
amongst tall pine   before the raped woman
housed entire nations within her ribcage
    from this place she became mountain
    transformed to trickster
    returned to mountain's face
earth and woman recall masked men
    their lies   the distortion
    touch of dead fingers on living flesh
the moment the violation began
death followed daughters mutilation   stood
bathed in sunlight   claws embedded in vulva
he tore away at her beauty   devoured her
entrails   thirsted for more in his
frenzied cannibalism of woman's heart
    not satisfied he sought out
the youngest   still the hunger continued
    the feeding became a feast
yellow moon wailed stone mourned   cried
out to the night for the madness to cease
    implored that the banquet table be
destroyed that the masks fall away

that the monster be starved
instead the constellations wept and buried
womanhood in starlit tears

II

beneath her soles lay crushed bone
ash and dust held together by earth
blood riddled thoughts hurried skyward
she does not remember that once she loved
cannot find the memory in
which she loved others
her face emerged in the water she answered
in garbled profanity scarlet princess squaw
eyes filled with hate stared back
challenged her to live or die in this windswept
valley urged her to give in give up
surrender to the sharp taloned beast
clenched fists beat her to forget discard
passion mutilate womans landscape
destroy lineage empty memory filled basket
where heart sits on her knees she pounded her
reflection turned fingers of rage into chokehold
forced hand down throat tore out
entire history then threw her grandmothers
against jagged rock when her voice cried out
she ground it into the dark stain stood
back while the river of blood spread then
deepened her flailing arms weakened as the
current overcame her screams lungs caved in
resistance succumbed to her monsters
resilience died embraced by defeat

determination vanished under the
cover of turbulent clouds
she looked around for the final time only
to bear witness to her land being consumed
by fire

III

imprints
deep
imbedded in earth
story
a journey across twinned mountain
twinned heart
reminders of all life found in this
plush forest of self
woman within man
man inside woman
twinned spirit
a gathering in the hillsides of a country where woman
life
creation
are seen as one
a time when two spirits
one body and the beginning are remembered
ancient woman dance
ancient woman thought
ancient woman language
fire inside minds eye
voice housed within ribcage of all beings who
walk this forest floor
shape changer

she/he
past and future sheltered by memory
war is foreign
not an option
twinned stone knows
understands
called woman home
brought her to this opening
old woman
young woman
heart upon heart
vision upon vision
history gathered amongst tall cedar
aware of heralding change
determined to emerge whole
unfaltered
steadfast
story woman was never homeward bound
thought woman does not need to return
woman language not lost
twinned heart never disappeared
plush green hillsides bathed in sunlight
know this

Resistance

resistance is a woman
whose land is all on fire
perseverance and determination
are her daughters
she is a palestinian mother who
hands her children a legacy of
war together with the
weapons to fight in it
she is a black woman draped
in purple satin who strolls
down a runway allowing only
the clothes she wears to be sold
resistance is the absent native woman
who died at the hands of
a white artist
who lives inside herself
while thriving inside of me
resistance is a girl child who
witnesses her mother's death and
swears to survive no matter
where the hiding place
she is a woman beaten with hate
by the man she loves who
decides to escape to a world
where touch is sacred
she is a woman torn apart by
the barbed wire surrounding her home
who plots a way out
despite the consequences
resistance is every woman who

has ever considered taking up
arms writing a story leaving the abuse
saving her children or saving herself
she is every woman who dares
to stage a revolution complete a novel
be loved or change the world
resistance walks across a landscape
of fire accompanied by her daughter's
perseverance and determination

Beneath distortion

you have told your friends all about me / and absolutely
nothing at the same time / in the end i am worn down /
my emotions rubbing away at my joints / my movement is
restricted upon your passing through my doorframe / have
you forgotten who you are / spirit / flesh / a puzzle of pain-
ful memories / abandonment and desertion / or is it that
you have not yet discovered the shores of your own heart /
perhaps when you do you will wash up on the shores of
mine / beached and burning in the sun / in the meantime
take back your cleavers which dismember me from myself /
instead of tuning out my politics just leave the room /
what remains is more oxygen for my lungs expanding /
contracting with the panic i've got locked inside / run to
your friends / go on / only this time forget my spirituality /
give them my rage / wrap them in the blanket of my confu-
sion and pain / offer them the food of all of me / let them
drink my blood flowing with my fear / share a banquet
with your friends and eat portions from each part of my
body / then digest / if afterwards you feel nauseous you
have only touched on who i am / without blurred vision
and from the pages of an anthropological textbook/ nor
from a slanted perspective of who your authors would have
me be / no longer will i be your princess or your drunk /
then when i give myself to you leaving the room will no
longer be an option / and you will no longer be sitting on
my chest
discarding my body parts/

and dance they will

today on the hillsides of nicaragua el salvador
guatemala another body of a lover or relation
comes sliding down in the red mud body following
body heart following heart careening downwards
only spirits find release as they fly into
the blue forming clouds above carcasses of
animals who have died through eating poisoned
flesh they picked away until white bone lay
exposed while charred skin flaked and
scattered across the landscape not even the
trees can grow from this deadly fertilizer
overhead the dead take off their masks
revealing the faces of my relatives and i am dragged
screaming back to my place of remembering
you cannot tell the clouds from the smoke my
sister from yours your child from my own our
mothers have the same name our fathers the same
tears all of them are huddled together in
the clearing their bones entwined with each
others finally they speak in unison no hills
stand in the way now no rivers left to cross
this last stand is the very solidarity they
lived and died for and yes you can burn
bodies and bury the skeletons but the clouds
you cannot stop their flight or put out
their form you can only watch as they take
off their masks and dance and dance they will

On this night, in this time of war

I

My pen has become my confidante
I know this because it is with
this instrument - I am the most - intimate.
Ink has become my medium
as I sit up on late nights such as this,
when sleep is evasive and my thoughts
dance to their own rhythm.
My words are my weapon
and it is with them I make change
from my crouched position in this time of war.

II

Tonight I will confidently hold my pen
as if it were my lover
who I do not want to let go of,
who I need to hold close to me for
a few more moments in time.
I will allow my desperation to express that if
it rests I do not know when we will
be together again, or when we might in secret
meet and exchange our affections.

III

The ink on this page is indented into
my mind and I will recognize the colour next time,
its intensity and solidness.

Perhaps it is going to be red, or black,
not this blue which reminds me of women and
the sky that wraps me in her arms during the day.
If it becomes red I will know to remember the
blood of my sisters, the healing and protection
we offer to one another. Black for the serenity
I am given during the hours when those
who wish me dead need to lay down
their weapons and gather enough strength
to face me and all my opposition to their
generous offers of further genocide.

IV

On this night I will house my words
in a lodge where they will be safe and
remain truthful. In this place, in this
time of war, I ask only that I respect
their meanings, use them only to make
change and that they hit their mark.

beloved

a chilling wind blows
down from the mountains
    my home no longer warm
death has taken my favourite chair
sits   stares   hollow cheeked
across frozen landscape
known as heart
    slow smile of grim reaper
spark of life in dead eyes
laughter escapes through rotting lips
    fear has replaced whatever laughter
ever filled my kitchen   voices now drowned
by their own silence
fury of snow dances with wind
    waits patiently to capture
a new victim   unsuspecting   careless
there are no angels
    christ offers no comfort
    god has turned his back   see him tremble
in terror   afraid it could be him
there is no justice
    this is not just
    the meek die violently
    the humble are trampled
my home is cold now
empty of laughter
demons are having a dinner party

at my table   this is the feast
of souls   young   old   female   male

a banquet prepared for the dying
everyone is invited to taste the flesh
    see how death sits comfortably
in my favourite chair by the window
    hear me howl into the night
    a wailing song for my beloved
    see me pound my fists against earth
    watch my rage thrown to the sky
    where wind will carry it into memory
wailing songs have no beginning
there is no end
you are forever
my beloved

Journey

walk across this crystal lake of my heart
        across my landscape sung to by loon
find yourself in the dancing shadows
        see your reflection at waters edge
roam my valleys in search of self
        come over to the other side of darkness
see the cavity of my vulva
        find the other world it opens into
hear the moon singing her lament
        you must dance or she will stop
watch the clouds for their vision
        or lose their words forever
lie across the smoothness of my back
        listen to the stories engraved in my heart
swim in the depths of my blood
        wash the wounds of your hardened insides
listen to my words   their light   my song
        they are for you   my beloved

Civilization

old buildings stand abandoned skyline juts
into purple grey haze vacant eyes
search a dust filled horizon construction hats
sit on distorted minds while handshakes mark the
beginning of the end in the distance god's house
sits empty steeples outstretched he left
before he answered anyones prayers smug in his deception
limb by limb bodies are torn crowds gather to
witness the death while blue mountains roll
in the background mourning song escapes through a
saxophone low and macabre wailing into the night
stone is cut against its grain men calculate its
stress level certain it contains no life certain
it can withstand the slaughter naked steel begins
the surgery the body collapses a throne is born
terror filled streets replace fields of tall grass
computer graphics spit out thought in this society
creativity is against the law push the buttons take
the credit accept the award for following the print
out step by step graphics roll onto the floor step on them
terror filled streets replace fields of tall grass
in my panic to survive the holocaust i managed to
find the rolling mountains managed to hide from
the soldiers having discovered my name on the most
wanted list having made the decision i am too
young to die

Black hands

tonight in a vortex of darkness
i watched your blood flow into
the walls of a crystal lined cave
inside this moment you became
the movement of jagged rock
your lungs created a dance of fine
sand floating skyward in a cloud of dust
i searched for your cave
inside my dreams
i looked within a hole whose
darkness fell off a cliff edge
then into your story
i have often wondered if the low rumble
of a moving earth was your song
whether the wail heard high in the
mountains belonged to you
or the lined face of a black stone
found at the mouth of a river
was you journeying towards the quiet place
between the stream of light
and the blanket of darkness

Do you remember

do you remember
how the song of a full moon
made you feel
when she roamed across your skin
then wove herself into a dream
do you remember
how the rhythm of language
transformed herself into a tapestry
that stretched across the mountain range
sleeping outside your cedar root home
do you remember
how you balanced on the tip
of a quarter moon
then gave birth to a star
who blazed your story into the eye of meteor
do you remember
how you rumbled inside a dark vortex
then with the splintered light
shifted the universe on her axis
do you remember
how you whispered of solitude
then found the moving line
between the underworld and skies blanket
do you remember
how you placed thought
inside a crystal lined cave
then leapt off the cliff into the light
do you remember
how you called on grandmother
then listened for her voice which

fell into your hand in a tear of rain
do you remember
how you wandered into the
arms of a hurricane
then discovered
    a moment of
    absolute silence
    where colour and sound
    meet to create a song

dedicated to Jeanette Armstrong in return for her poetry...

Dream

last night you drummed me Azania
i heard her shores and felt her lap against my heart
beating
            beating
                        deep into the night
you brought me to the edge of her forests into
a clearing down into the opening i walked towards
women gathered in a circle renewal of spirits a
dance to celebrate your survival a dance of masks
you drummed me Azania on a taut skin
the colour of my own down from the mountains your
voices travelled on bolts of lightning touching
down on moist earth
beating
      beating
                  and you raise your arms to the sky
your chanting grows stronger as your bodies move to
and fro colliding with the old women you honour
through your struggle
beating
      beating
                  and your hands touch one another
                  touch the earth
                  touch me
last night you drummed me Azania deep into the night
taking me to her hills and a circle of women whose
outstretched arms embraced me and

beating
beating
your spirit met mine and
we celebrated
beating
beating
you drummed me Azania

dedicated to Thato Bereng

Distances

last night
deep in the
womb of
mother earth
my prayers
for you
whispered to
my grandmothers
were
answered.
on this night
the spirits
will protect
you
in ways
i cannot.
pull those blankets
closer
to
your
woman's skin,
wrap ourself
in blankets
of snow
under skies of
woman's colour
and once,
only once,
acknowledge the
spirits

who will
watch over you
in ways i
cannot while
so many miles
away.
know they
are strong
and willing
to protect
you
in this
your most
vulnerable state.
on this
night
touch my
hair
as i too,
wrap myself
in blankets
of snow

dedicated to Grace Channer

untitled memory

she conjured sensuous mist
moaned her way across my skin
left a trail of blue and green
within my eyelids
she moved forest
into a mime of wordless sound
a symphony of body where touch
translates into perfect being
left a trail of story
embodied in the voice of earth
her timeless heart whirled the clouds
into a journey where new
movement created spirit
her translucent body spoke
of how shaded blue and green
are one inside the other
she whispered her secrets of origin
in tones of invisible touch
she carried a newborn star homeward
then settled against the brown
of her sister

awakening

where were you during the night
of drifting stars who wept salt tears
were you caught in the same place
somewhere between home and the barren moon
i called to you while i dreamt
of an awakened faceless phantom
whose name i no longer recall in any language
yet whose eyes twinkle with unspoken secrets
where were you when at the rivers edge
i danced to my wordless song while
my body became a fish swimming upstream
were you that silent shadow cast
across my scaled thoughts which searched for meaning
while others blindly wandered past the moving tide
were you the one who chanted deep within the mountain
while i turned inside to revive
my memory of you where before the darkness
we lived inside a cave of light

dedicated to Shelly

the revolution of not vanishing

i sit here and read your work
    the colour of your words
    the shape of your heart
alone i follow the lines captured
between the spaces of letters   i
stop when there is a dark dot   but
only to gulp in the breath needed
for me to continue   i fall off the
page when a gap appears into a
lake of salt water tears and i
swim its length i re-emerge when
each new sentence begins ready to
follow the path you have bulldozed through
the jungles of this city   this place
that is not a home   my legs give way
and i am on my knees   my blood splatters onto
the ground while more gravel embeds
itself into my flesh   i weep torrents
of water creating an ocean now as
i am taken to my place of remembering
    while anger and resistance become sisters
    while i journey towards sunlight   i run
into the border of a blank white square
and celebrate
        and i celebrate
        to the drumbeat
        resounding out of
        the skin of your heart
        then i dance

dedicated to Chrystos

Inside this moment

autumn crept onto my back
from here she turned herself
into multiple orange and brown
from here she could see
where the wind would take her
a blanket of leaves became my coat
while on my head i wrapped a snowdrift
i walked through a deserted park
towards my winter mountains
along the way we met
along the way we danced an
honour song for each other
an honour song whose tune was womanly blue
whose words were the shape of memory
our feet became roots burrowed in brown earth
our thoughts were the first snowfall
do you remember how in becoming light
you found your freedom between two worlds
how in this moment we sung all our memory
as we etched our life into a constellation
remember to pull the blanket close
to wrap yourself within a snowdrift
remember your honour song is carved
into my heart and that each time
i look skyward i hear its rhythm
then dance upon a snow covered field
alone in your universe

dedicated to Michael Smith 1957-1991

Homeward bound

distance at this point
in time
has no definition
except for
what idle
minds
choose to create
i can say this now
because tonight
while the wind
howls outside
your window
i will silently
creep into our
bedroom and
share with you
my friend
a night of lovemaking
and passion that
distance cannot prevent
while gusts of snow
swirl against the
glass pane facing east
i will quietly
whisper a prayer
for your protection
during journeys made
while sleeping on
roads that are new

and tracks that
will guide you safely home
where you will rest
your head on my shoulder
and speak of how
close we are
despite the prairies
that separate my
hand from holding
yours

dedicated to Grace

Betty

i did not know that spirits
can bleed yours reaffirms
that rivers are created
by our blood as you lie
bleeding through 56
stab wounds the flow
leads to the ocean of my heart
and in it i swim spawning with
my sisters going against the
tide if i follow its direction
long enough i imagine that i too
will wash up on the shores
of another woman's heart

this bearing witness to
our rebirth is painful to
partake in the journey
is over terrain strewn with
sharp rocks and my feet
are covered with open
wounds my knees well
scarred

there are those who believe
that our destination has
been arrived at when we lay
in the rivers of our own blood
drowning in front of their
eyes others still who
imagine it all to have ended

when the first stab was
inflicted

i on the other hand
know that rivers lead to oceans
and that landslides of red mud
stop at the base of trees
whose arms reach to the sky while
living amongst tall grass and
the fireweed which has survived
many blazes

your death   my friend   marked
my renewal and aided the survival
of us who remain behind   i
have seen you on every street
corner   i have been you each
time i lived through the abuse
inflicted upon my body and
spirit by men   i remain you
as i am caught up in the
currents of your blood   i
bring you forward with me every
time i dance amongst the smoke
and fireweed   celebrating
our continued existence

i know that rivers lead to
oceans   that fireweed never
dies   that i will sing
your name into the wind as
you wash up on the shores

of my heart
time and time
again

dedicated to Helen Betty Osborne

Directions of change

it is the rage
locked between the boulders
of our hearts that
forces madness to
propel us shakily forward
into unknown futures
filled with promises
and no guarantees
besides the rage
there is our love
and our belief that
struggle no matter how
painful is worthy of
looking into and considering
if we are to survive on
the streets and behind the
doors of a house we have
chosen to call home

at night the warmth
found between the cotton
sheets of our bed
can quietly slip out
of the window leaving
in its wake tidal waves
of anxiety concerning
the tomorrow we have
so often structured our
days around instead the
salt of our tears erodes

away the flesh of our open
wounds while the sting causes
our eyes to close and our
hearts to become
battlegrounds of change

Sunsets

Sunsets are reminders that,
In this life, sanctuary is
Only for the privileged whites
Who we discovered in 1492. Instead
Its warm rays touch only those
Who are prepared to receive its heat
Without the desire to control
Its directions. I know this now
Through having forgotten
The landscape of the home of
My people. Through having moved
To the city where daylight is
Controlled by streetlights,
Where daily isolation is a fact
Of life to others born of
The earth now ravaged by fire.
Serving no purpose concrete,
Asphalt and steel girders longing
To touch the clouds receive no
Warmth, other than through the
Bodies of those who cannot and
Will not succumb to the whims of
A society that holds no place
For them, yet gives permission
For their deaths, frozen whilst
Asleep dreaming of far off lands
They once travelled from in
Order to get to this place. I
Know now that sunsets are
Only for those who live and

Die in the struggle to receive
Its warmth, without claiming
Ownership to its messages,
That the stroking of our bodies
By its generous fingertips is
Never to be taken for granted,
Nor forgotten. For loss of language
Implies firstly
Then ensures secondly,
Certain death.

This is not a metaphor

today from romania there were pictures released
        photographs brought across the ocean images
children trapped between a fascist regime and resistance
        most of them were my son's age
        though I could see five and six year olds
I looked closer falling into their eyes   looked at
scars on their heads as the result of experiments
        each body was starved   most had no clothes on
and what was there was torn and blood riddled
        the bodies I had seen before   starving children
seem so common-place   poverty a given   I looked into
the eyes of a child and saw nazi germany   starvation is
a blank look   rags offer little warmth   I searched my
memory and found nothing to compare   crouched in a
corner   shaking so hard I expected to hear bones
rattle   a child cowarded as if she   he could escape
the probing camera   I recall the names given to me
        my anger in response I look back into my childhood a
beating
could feel gentle depending how hard I was hit   my sons
tears yesterday at being called halfbreed   still
I find nothing that screams the terror carried by
the mute child   wide eyed and starved
        I looked farther back   across the landscape of my history
according to the books   as told by white colonizers I look
into the effects of columbus being lost and
find the truth   it is not me that is savage
        or primitive   or doomed to your hell   it is not me
that takes the spirits of her children and replaces it
with terror   it will not be me
who takes responsibility for your savagery

I have not gone

in my youth
i recall my mother's
hands cradling my
body into a dark night
her palm roamed
through my hair
planted story on the
insides of my eyes
fingertips whispered
of my beginnings
spoke of how joy
and i were one
calloused hands
worn by time
worn by cold
cracked into the shape
of mountains face
hands that brought me
back to my place
of solitude
then took me forward
to the places where
hatred could not exist
hands that opened
my heart to the
sound of water
touching stone
stone
stone's voice
cradled within my mother's hands

mother
returning
returning
to the warmth
of your hands

dedicated to Helen Betty Osborne

Turtle woman

I

i can hear the seeds inside rattling.
when the sound begins i can feel
a warmth envelop my body.
my insides are the seeds.

II

shaking, shaking,
rocking my soul....
the rattle is what
witnesses my departure,
the rattle welcomes
my return....
her voice weaves her
words around my body.
shaking, shaking,
rocking on the insides
of my soul.

III

she would have it i
leave my physical being
to travel through the
tunnel of myself.

IV

my rattle speaks to me
during the night.
she tells me a story about
herself when she was young,
the change she has bore
witness to, bringing the past
and present to become sisters.
if one listens carefully, takes
her messages in through the heart,
stories are heard.
healing stories.

V

the story of the rattle goes on....

VI

the songs of the turtle have always
been here and they will be sung
far into the future. they will always
speak truth, always mourn and celebrate....

VII

sing your tones of light
and into yourself you will
travel, deep into your beginnings
back to your place of remembering.

VIII

the sound of the seeds goes on,
forward into time and space...
there are voices in this room,
women talking. the rattling goes on...

IX

this shell houses her spirit,
the sound of her innards gets louder
as her words are formed....her words
are gentle and rock
the insides of my soul.

X

not one rattle is the same.
not one woman's make-up
is as another. our masks change
and how we take them off is
not done in any one way. i watch
as mine fall away, i celebrate
another woman's removal of hers.

XI

i placed my spirit inside my rattle and danced...

XII

the stories of the rattle thunder
on....sometimes loudly, at other
times in soft tones....if one
listens carefully it talks from
the insides of their souls...
all the joy and pain of our
lives can be heard when she sings.

XIII

the story of the rattle continues....forward into time....

Stones memory

translucent stone murmured of my beginnings
whispered the secrets of my origins
called me home following nights of darkness
cried out for my return to sunlight
urged me to bring memory forward
compelled my circle to become complete
round curve of mountain's face
showed herself to me in a blanket
of blue and green expression
stories passed from palm to palm
trickled down my throat
etched their essence upon my heart
embedded their words within my ribcage
settled amongst my blood
i remember her face
recall her tone
i remember my relatives
their journey from water to land
i am reminded of every stone
who has ever spoken
ever wailed
ever celebrated
every stone whose birth
is evidence of creation
whose death harbours
new journeys on wind's voice
i remember every stone
i have swallowed
 every stone i have
 ever held

every stone that
has crossed my path
and cleared the way
footprints

beyond the plush green embankment
the smooth body of sand touches the
fingertips of water
here there are no words
just sound in constant motion
caught in a place between
the blue and brown
here too exists the voice inside of colour
they are whispering secrets to me
as i dash across the earth
i am determined to find the
exact moment and place where
sound birthed song

Driftwoodwoman

buried under a mountain of her own victimization
grabbing at sun covered by her distorted thought
caught by her reflection in a cracked mirror
veiled in drifting spiderwebs
unable to hear the voice of spiderwoman
unyielding to the rhythm of thoughtwoman
a prisoner by her own conviction
beyond her cement walls
a gathering of women tend the fire
calling her home
calling her home

of ice and rain

she stood draped in silence, imagined that if she listened intently she would hear the echo of words. they were cradled in her palm, small children whose mouths burned with the unspoken, old women tired by not having been heard, men wrapped in their own verbal confusion unable to reach expression. the flame moved toward its own fury as she looked into transparent blue. the dance started to heighten as slowly words took shape. they slipped out of her grasp, took their first breath. ignited by their desire for meaning they moved gracefully to the earth. drop upon drop spiralled outward, circle within circle formed into the language of ice and rain. left behind warmth returned to her hand as life danced around her reflection.

Stones journey

through mist stone woman trickled
settled inside   gave birth to her daughters
story enfolded by lineagebound by memory
careened forward by past movement
within her caves engravings traced her history
each footstep embedded in stone
she remembered her grandmothers   their trail of tears
oceans left by woman's journey   she recalled
the beginning   the shape changer she became
she saw color evolve into tomorrow   she
remembered the birth of water   her two
spirits   their perfect solitude with creation
stone woman wandered beneath darkness   her translucent
mauve shifted between stars   in one motion
she draped her flesh across a wavering
horizon   gave life to meteor   jagged rock
spoke with her in gentle tone of
purple song   from where she rested water
spirit   held in the palm of solitude   had
always been   here there were no
words except those found within the stars   those
whirled by the hands of color   those
whispered through the night   caught between
the sun   moon and the underworld

Dedicated to Susan and Tanis

Bound by wind

words congested block passages to universes
sometimes seen gleaming through the clouds
during early hours of mornings enshrouded
in mist, encased in dewdrops sprinkled
lightly underfoot. obstructions stopping
ones thought journeys cause uneasiness
in hearts surrounded by inadequate
vocabulary, causing spirits to fold
bodies into fetus positions, lying
beneath clean sheets, heads resting on
much used pillows.
sensations of expression are as necessary
to ones survival as open fields under clear
skies, rolling with stalks of tall
sweetgrass and scents of cedar and pine.
so i write and travel on the wings of
sound waves which will carry me to the
tops of mountains, enabling me to
speak with my grandmothers.
from here i will return with the
landscape of a heart surrounded by
those very pine trees that eluded
me in the distance. from the rock where
visions are given i will return with
the smell of sweetgrass in my hair,
carrying branches of cedar out of which
i will make a bed for my words. on these
nights when sleep escapes me i will
again take flight and return being able
to say

i have come down from the mountains
having gathered strength from her forests
and insight from her clear waters,
caught now in free-flight on winds from the east,
wound in spring landslides of new movement.

Stone woman

creation began when stone
rolled down my throat
found her way to my stomach
and gave birth to herself
late into the darkness
she crept into my dreams
excited to have found me
lying beneath moon's face
while caught on the wind
of a journey through time
the stories on her face
revealed her history and
brought mine back into
the forefront of my existence

homeward

she falls softly
upon ancient brown
spiralling her way home
moving pass the present
toward her yesterdays
slow descent
through blinking pathway
worn by her mother
travelled by her grandmother
her movement decisive
she returns to her beginning

Having been home

I speak to you now
As a lover would.
Your hills have
Touched my core,
Normally surrounded by
Asphalt and fumes
Of poison. Gently rolling
Across your curves in
A bus I promise
To return by foot,
Carried by the wheels
Of a car, accompanied next
Time by a companion
Known as my son.

Slowly we will follow paths
Made by women, my
Grandmothers,
To sacred grounds
Where rays of sun
Transform wartorn bodies,
Ravaged by time and struggle,
And from where we can emerge
Healed though scarred from
Flesh wounds. (reminders of
where we have been and what we can expect)

Having been home this one
Time memories remain,
Etched in vision brought

During nights of cold sweats,
Carried on tears from centuries
Of pain and of having to
Go into unknown times which
Guarantee a future not known
To my generation, but promised
To my sons.

Having been home this one time
Return is imminent and I will
Bring my child into the
Arbour for safety and we
Will roll across your flesh
Wounds, reminders of
Where we have been and
What we have survived.

We remember

We live
    within the fine line
    between the underworld and the sky
We have been here
    since Thought Being
    gave birth to shape
We have no choice
    but to listen to the voices
    caught between our
    joints as they struggle
    towards sunlight
We will know
    when it is time
    by the movement
    birthed within our ribcage
We have not forgotten
    our journey
    towards this moment

Earthly beauty

I have wandered across moons face
I understand why she keeps her distance
she refuses to be a part of the destruction
I have swum through the deepest waters
I know what she hides in the ocean bed
the unscathed secrets of the other world
I have leapt off the highest cliff's edge
I understand now what the darkness hides
that within splintered light exists blazing truth
I have spoken with original being
I understand that in the end
we are left with nothing
short of new beginnings

dedicated to Ruby Martin

survival through the sacred

the revolution you speak of
inside a house unlike any other
is shaded by mauve spiralling skybound
within these walls fire
colours your resistance while
sacred being rests in an arbour
there is no shimmering steel
or the whirl of bullets
instead you ride on
the voice of thunder
travelling inside the wind
to your place of remembering
you are that erupting volcano of
molten red crawling earthbound
to your secret place where
revolution occurs with every
cloud you inhale
every ocean you birth
every moment that passes
when you could have died
and become that sleepy mountain
on the blazing horizon of tomorrow

dedicated to Joy Harjo, Oklahoma, 1992

Perfect solitude

in "perfect solitude" i
walk in silence through
my corridors
        an early morning
journey through the mist
of my past in which
each step brings me
further into memory
deeper into my lineage

water laps
against the shores of
my heart
conversation
with self
despite there being
no words
        into my depths i plunge
and see countless women
each one of
two hearts
each one in
"perfect solitude"
memory has no time frame
comes from not one place
lineage surrounds me
surrounds these
women. water creation
against the shores of
my heart i have

given life to
endless memory
and in countless
directions i travel

space has no meaning
instead i free fall
into my yesterdays
and my tomorrow
bound by my vision
of a world where
"perfect solitude"
two hearted women
and creation
are seen as one
lineage and memory are not
separate in my waters
creation is possible only through
the renewal and recognition
of both

"perfect solitude" — this concept was initially voiced by Columpa Bobb's "solitude" and developed further by Lee Maracle as "perfect solitude". This is a concept Native cultures hold in common with one another in its relationship to "perfect" and "being". In my mind, "perfect solitude" expresses oneness with creation; oneness with self.

Reconciliation

I

words create images
unlike the pictures
of memories formed
in my mind while sleeping
    recollections   thoughts
spaces unoccupied by this
body encompassing spirits
    conversations interactions
face these eyes
never held in their sights
while awake
    memories formed through
links with spirits from another time
    woman   you who has
entered the iris at
the center of my soul
held me one night
while howling outside
my window the wind
told me stories
    of who your are
and whispered the secrets
of where i come from
    your hands touch my skin
and weave roots between
our bodies
woman   your hair touched
the nape of my neck

while tears slowly crawl down
these cheeks that cover bone
        strands find their way
to my breasts
(and like lovers we
become intimate)
        your hands are strong
their strokes on my shoulders
remind me of waves
        freeflowing   hitting shores
of sand   they pound against my
flesh   each movement
catches my eye
        i long to capture spaces
in time like these moments
when in sleep you visit
        women from
whose roots i come

II

while sitting cross-legged
in the lodge
you visited me on a
gust of wind blown
through the western doorway
        had i known you could
travel at will i would
have been vigilant
much earlier
        while still a child i stopped
searching

for your arrival   having run out of patience
        to stare into the ocean of water
i lived near became
simply
too dangerous
        according to some i may have
been swallowed up as the
water parted   engulfing my soul
on an endless journey of
day-dreams   stargazing   visions
        so when you blew in from the west
i was caught unaware   surprised
        from the doorway you
entered taking the form of
the buffalo   your fur was old
        generations   and your nostrils dripped
moisture due to the heat   electricity
        vibrancy in the air and in our hearts
        your frame was larger in size
then i imagined it to be
        yet outside of skin you
did not cease to grow
        around the sacred fire you
dance   intrigued by its flames
        mesmerized by its warmth
        nose to the ground
you draw close to me and i
am shocked at my childlike enchantment
        sitting next to you i hear your
laughter resounding beneath canvas
walls erected to keep the rain outside
        you whisper in my ear you are glad

i came
and knowing to look sideways
for you would create an empty space
my eyes remain focused on the fire
your voice is familiar   its tone
the same as in childhood dreams
closing my eyes i picture your face
old   wrinkled and worn by time
the corners of your eyes frozen in laughter
surrounded by lines only pain
could have imprinted
mouth set in a position not disclosing
thoughts being formed in your mind
you slowly give me a secretive smile
my eyelids open at the point when
the chanting begins
high pitched you join in
placing your mouth close to my ear so
i cannot misunderstand words carried
through air   breath touches my lobe
encouraging the tears already balanced
in my eyes   perpetuating my
longings for you
noticing the buffalo being herded out
through the doorway i glance
to my left the air is on fire
in flames and i know you
must leave my side
canvas flaps loudly as you
move in a circle around
the fire towards the exit
once   before moving on you

while silently i offer gratitudes
that are inadequate for gifts received
   removal of hands takes with them
my years of pain   isolation when we
no longer spoke late at night
   evenings when the wind stopped
bringing to me your chants
   slowly i rise   following your
footsteps though not catching
in my vision their imprints

III

cool breezes blow my way
this quiet evening
bringing on its breath images
of your face
   with me now i place my
head gently between your breasts
   gentle curves remind me of
earth beneath feet
   hands caress me and flow
of water is heard
   blood passes between us
strong now
beyond control
   skin ripples
   movement created by motion
not known before
   read a poem about cherokee eden*
strawberries are
   abundant

offered between hearts
reconciliation
reaffirming strengths through bonding
i am familiar with this fruit
many times i have prepared a
ceramic bowl overflowing with
slashes of red swirling through
air as i pass to you
what is yours
then mine
reconciliation...occurrences following
absence   longings   fitting for homecoming
curtains caught on a gust of air
speak in tune with your arrival
placement of hands on face
you have been absent
beyond time frames though you are
as familiar to this body as is
the rhythm of your voice
thighs entwine and i long
to enter you
unite   soar in freeflight
as we once did
you
woman
alone in dark places
have met with me your daughter
in mid-air collision on each full moon
mother who has given birth
to me painfully
to whom i owe my roots
leave silently

to whom i owe my roots
leave silently
as the rain increases
covering your tracks
behind your back
cherokee eden
strawberries
reconciliation
remain in place for when
you return
to stay

**Marilou Awiakta wrote a piece "Cherokee Eden: An Alternative to the Apple" in which she says:*
"Reconciliation. Healing. Acceptance of the human tendency to quarrel. A pattern for restoring harmony that involves mutual responsibility and restitution. This is Cherokee Eden, the powerful medicine of the strawberry."
I use my reference to remember this myth that has been around for 35,000 years; to remember what reconciliation means in my life.
To my mother who I have seen only in my dreams for a memory I cannot recall yet to whom I am grateful to, always, for the choices she left open to me. The woman who, painfully, gave birth to me. Meegwetch Mother. Reconciliation and a bowl of the ripest strawberries...

Connie Fife

i write who i am; from my perspective as well as from the place most people would like me to stay. ink flows to paper slowly, sometimes painfully, for as an indian lesbian living in a racist, homophobic society there will always be people who wish to keep me silenced. so.... when i am quiet it is not because i am allowing myself to be further victimised, but rather i, too, await my own eruptions.

SISTER VISION PRESS

Sister Vision: Black Women and Women of Colour Press was founded by Women of Colour in 1985 and is run and controlled by Women of Colour. Sister Vision's mandate and priority is publishing books by Black women, First Nations women, Asian women and women of mixed racial heritage.

The vision of the Press came out of a need for autonomy, our need to determine the context and style of our work and to control the words and images that are produced about us.

Our books have proven to be a powerful vehicle for challenging sexism, heterosexim in our respective communities and racism, bias and prejudice in Euro-Centric communities.

We continue our vision to publish emerging writers of colour, as well as established writers and to act as a cultural and political literary force.

A free catalogue of our books is available on request.

You can buy Sister Vision titles at your bookstore, or order them directly from the publisher (P.O. Box 217, Station E, Toronto, Ontario, Canada, M6H 4E2) Phone 416-533-2184

Please include $3.00 postage for the first book and $.50 for each additional book.